D1121516

Walla W...
County Librar...

GYMNASTICS TIME!

by Brendan Flynn

BUMBA BOOKS™

LERNER PUBLICATIONS ◆ MINNEAPOLIS

Note to Educators:

Throughout this book, you'll find critical thinking questions. These can be used to engage young readers in thinking critically about the topic and in using the text and photos to do so.

Lerner Publications Company
A division of Lerner Publishing Group, Inc.
241 First Avenue North
Minneapolis, MN 55401 USA

For reading levels and more information, look up this title at www.lernerbooks.com.

Library of Congress Cataloging-in-Publication Data

Names: Flynn, Brendan, 1977–
Title: Gymnastics time! / by Brendan Flynn.
Description: Minneapolis : Lerner Publications, [2017] | Series: Bumba books—Sports Time! | Includes bibliographical references and index.
Identifiers: LCCN 2016001069 (print) | LCCN 2016005882 (ebook) | ISBN 9781512414363 (lb : alk. paper) | ISBN 9781512415476 (pb : alk. paper) | ISBN 9781512415483 (eb pdf)
Subjects: LCSH: Gymnastics—Juvenile literature.
Classification: LCC GV461.3 .F59 2017 (print) | LCC GV461.3 (ebook) | DDC 796.44—dc23

LC record available at http://lccn.loc.gov/2016001069

Manufactured in the United States of America
1 – VP – 7/15/16

Expand learning beyond the printed book. Download free, complementary educational resources for this book from our website, www.lernerresource.com.

Table of Contents

Fun with Gymnastics

Gymnastics is a fun indoor sport.

Kids of all ages like to play.

You do not need your

own equipment.

You can join a club.

Your school may have

equipment too.

You need comfortable clothes.

You also need a mat.

Some gymnasts use music too.

Why might comfortable clothes be helpful?

Start by warming up.

Stretching is important.

You need to be flexible and strong.

Why do you need to be flexible?

You can practice tumbling

on the mats.

You can walk on the

balance beam.

Older kids jump from
the vault.

They swing from the bars.

They fly high in the air!

Safety is important.

A spotter helps with tricky moves.

How do you think a spotter helps with safety?

You can watch gymnastics

on TV.

Some schools have teams.

JANSSEN·FRITSEN

Kids have fun in gymnastics.

It is a great way to stay in shape.

Gymnastics Equipment

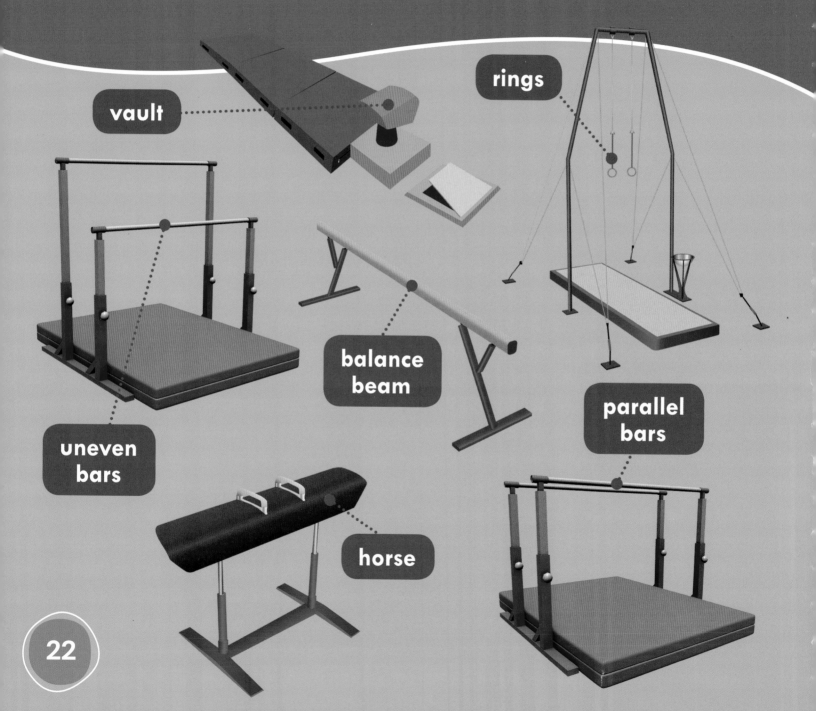

vault

rings

uneven bars

balance beam

parallel bars

horse

Picture Glossary

balance beam

a narrow piece of wood that gymnasts perform on

flexible

able to bend easily

spotter

a person who helps with hard moves

vault

a piece of equipment that gymnasts bounce off and jump over

23

Index

Read More

Borth, Teddy. *Gymnastics: Great Moments, Records, and Facts.* Minneapolis: Abdo Kids, 2015.

Karapetkova, Holly. *Gymnastics.* Vero Beach, FL: Rourke, 2010.

Morey, Allan. *Gymnastics.* Minneapolis: Bullfrog Books, 2015.

Photo Credits